Summary: The Hillbilly Elegy: A Memoir of a Family and Culture in Crisis

Key Takeaways and Analysis

By J.D. Vance

Busy Reader

Copyright
© 2017 by Busy Reader

Table of Content

Introduction

A young couple – J.D. Vance's grandparents – migrated from the hills of Kentucky to Ohio shortly after World War II to move up the socioeconomic ladder. In search of a better life, they tried to escape poverty and almost everything behind except for their Appalachian habits and values. Some were wonderfully positive, such as loyalty and love of country. But others like alcohol abuse, violence, and instability had also been woven into the fabric of their lives.

Violent as they may seem and in a town where many children don't finish high school and vices are not out of the norm, they raised a grandson who managed defying tremendous odds. The only reason why J.D. withstood such system was because Papaw and Mamaw eventually reconciled, becoming his unofficial guardians. In scenes at once harrowing and hilarious, we come to know these loud, rowdy gun-toters as the loyal and loving family whose encouragement helped the author endure "decades of chaos and heartbreak."

Hillbilly Elegy is a book that demonstrates the full measure of the brokenness that wracks Appalachia, but it is also a story that exemplifies the depths of familial love and opportunity.

ONE

A Home on the Hills

Although J.D. grew up living with his mother and sister, he always knew where he belonged, up on the hills with his extended family on his mother's side – the Blantons. The Blanton's were from Jackson, Kentucky – a small mountain-town in the heart of coal country and deeply steeped in the Appalachian culture.

The mountains provided a scenic backdrop for J.D.'s happiest childhood memories with his grandparents, Papaw and Mamaw, in the picture. They did their best to keep him from the worst of their family. Mamaw was best known as the toughest woman in town. She always ensured that he never witnessed any of his mother's drama and the problems she caused during her occasional visits.

J.D.'s grandparents eventually left Jackson and settled in Middletown, Ohio to escape all the poverty and vices. He still went to Jackson every now and then to visit his ailing great-grandmother. He and his cousins would run free in the nearby mountains, oblivious of the poverty that surrounded them and his great-grandmother's deteriorating health.

Jackson bred the fiercest yet uncompromisingly loving people with a deeply-embedded Appalachian culture. They respected the dead and helped others in need. However, it had its fair share of problems too. There was sort of people who shirked work and made excuses for everything. In addition to the struggles of this poverty-stricken town, a drug addiction took root. The educational system was deteriorating as well because poor parents could not afford a better option but to send their children to the terrible schools regardless.

When J.D. was young, he genuinely appreciated the place he called home and he had a deep sense of pride towards his family. But as the years went by, the painful reality became clear to him that people were suffering because they were not doing anything to make their difficult situation better.

J.D. met a lot of people in his youth, some were mean and extremely reticent about their problems. Many of them were in poor health and could not afford the treatment they needed to improve their well-being. In fear of judgment, they either avoid those discussions or deny their health issues. A study was made on the local teens which inspired them to ignore their problems and the uncomfortable truths at such a young age. As a result, they tend to put the blame on other things such as political situation, other people and the list goes on. Rather than finding a solution, they made up an "alternate reality" where, according to them, problems are nonexistent. This defense mechanism provides a resilience to hardship, but also makes it impossible to look at oneself honestly.

TWO

A New Refuge for a Better Life

Despite of the chaos and mess that surrounded J.D.'s life, he was well-sustained by his grandparents' support and life lessons. They devoted their maximum efforts to giving J.D. the best shot to live the American Dream, something they did not achieve.

The story of his grandparents' courtship, and their migration from Kentucky to Ohio, was one that had been handed down through the years as family lore. Mamaw became pregnant with her first child when she was just fourteen. To avoid further complications, she lied about her real age. With the hope of giving their growing family a better future, they moved from Jackson, Kentucky to Middletown, Ohio. Papaw quickly managed to land a job at Armco, a steel company that regularly hired applicants from Kentucky.

Although separated from their extended family, they found themselves in a familiar environment in their new refuge as other Kentuckians were migrating too. In spite of the familiarity, problems arose from both ends. Their family back in Kentucky expected Papaw and Mamaw to visit them often (regardless of their financial means). On the other hand, the white Ohioans were suspicious of the Appalachian migrants.

Notwithstanding the Vances' problems and challenges faced, they were able to adjust to their new lifestyle. Middleton was far different from Kentucky, and they focused on their work and did everything possible to make their lives better.

THREE

The Appalachians

Coming from an Appalachian descent, Papaw and Mamaw would occasionally display their Appalachian outburst particularly when a member of their family was being mistreated. An illustration of this was when a store owner scolded Jimmy for playing with an expensive toy. As a result, Papaw broke the toy into pieces while Mamaw threw random items off the shelves, cursing. Despite the fact that their outrage was beyond the norm, it didn't bother them at all and believed their behavior was completely normal. That incident clearly demonstrated the hillbilly way of life.

J.D.'s grandparents fulfilled each of their parental responsibilities in their own ways. Papaw worked on cars in his spare time, and Mamaw did her best to keep the family intact. Because of her protective instinct, she had a dream of becoming a children's lawyer but never pursued it as she lacked the opportunities to do so. As they had left Kentucky in exchange for a better life, they expected their children to make use of the head start and grab the opportunity they laid for them.

FOUR

Vance Family Troubles

Papaw and Mamaw had their first born, Jimmy, in 1951. They wanted to have more children even though Mamaw already had nine miscarriages. They finally gave up once they had three children. A while later, Papaw developed a drinking habit and his behavior began to change drastically.

His drinking habit had caused a lot of problems as he transformed to a violent person who even punched Mamaw in the eye in his rage. In return for his barbarity, Mamaw who had never drunk any alcohol had changed too and once smashed a vase on Papaw's head. They put on success as their facade, Papaw earned well; thus, were richer than their family back in Kentucky. But on the inside, their family was disintegrating. In addition to the misery, even Mamaw's brothers were supportive of Papaw's vices.

Mamaw was able to make new friends, but as the time went by, she began to withdraw and their neighborhood kids started to call her an "evil witch". The more Papaw drunk, the more she neglected her household responsibilities. Amidst the circumstances, their hillbilly culture became more dominant than ever. The couple would remain calm and go on with their lives but it took only a few seconds for them to become their usual violent selves. Mamaw loathed disloyalty to such extent that she counted it as a cardinal sin that the offender should be punished.

Papaw's vices continued and spent most of his nights drinking. Mamaw, on the other hand, found her new life's mission: to make him suffer in her own hands. One night when Papaw came home drunk, she doused his body with gasoline and threw a match on his chest. They continued this way of life until they witnessed its aftermath. Under such circumstances, their kids had a troubled childhood and suffered the consequences. They had issues when they came of age as they were deeply scarred. Although Jimmy and Lori did find their way, Bev – J.D.'s mother – who got pregnant when she was eighteen still bore the scars of her upbringing.

Papaw quit drinking and although they now lived separately, they spent a lot of time together. After they had seen the effects of their actions on their children, they did their best to heal the wounds they inflicted. From helping Lori break free from the bonds of her marriage to lending money to Bev for child welfare, they did everything they could to help their children. The couple who had failed their children in their youth had now devoted their lives to making up for it.

FIVE

Middletown's Disintegration and Social Decay

In his youth, J.D. believed that Middletown could be grouped into three geographical regions. The first part was the area in which the rich ones lived, especially the doctors; the second one where the poor people resided, mostly near Armco; lastly, where the Vances inhabited, and it housed factories and deserted warehouses. Although there was a fine line between this area and the one with the poorest, he wanted to believe that his family was above the poverty line.

As he grew up, the disintegration of Middletown became obvious to him. In spite of the town's beauty, it was possible to buy a house at a very low price. This change happened as the populations of the working-class – who inhabited neighborhoods with high poverty – began to rise. Even if the locals wanted to move, they usually could not afford the expense to do so. The ones who had the financial capabilities left the town, and the ones who had naught were trapped.

Armco later teamed up with Kawasaki, which meant that the Japanese company was giving Armco another chance and this provided the people to have a job. Unfortunately, the locals did not grab the opportunity as most parents did not want their children to become steel workers. Rather, many of them wanted their kids to pursue the American Dream, ironically, they were not willing to work hard for it.

Most of them did not think of having a higher education as an advantage, yet they wanted to achieve something big in their lives. Students slack in school because there is no one to convince them on how important education is. J.D., too, was rarely reprimanded for his poor performance. This attitude of negligence still continues today. Locals talk about industry and hard work, while oblivious of their own laziness. In reality, the formula for living the American Dream is they ought to have a higher education then become hard workers. But most hillbillies did otherwise.

SIX

J.D.'s Immediate Family

When J.D. was six, his mother had his name changed to erase the memory of his biological father. Although Bev did not attain a higher education, she helped her son with his projects and encouraged him to pursue higher education by constantly telling him that an education is always a blessing.

Mamaw also taught J.D. how to fight. The lesson's unspoken rule was one should never start a fight unless someone hurled insults at their family. This way of raising children was common among Appalachian people as the fierce defense of one's own was one of their undeniable traits. She also gave him tips on how to stand his ground if and when he needed to fight. Eventually,

J.D. had grown into a brave young man as he defended himself and the others from classroom bullies.

Clearly, Papaw and Mamaw were his best friends which provided a great support system in his life. But one day, things started to change as Bob – his stepfather – came, and he and Bev decided to move to Preble County. But, things did not go well. In addition to J.D.'s health problems and struggles in studying, his trauma because of the violence at home was starting to manifest. His mom even tried to kill herself, and immediately they were back in Middletown without his stepfather. She became more erratic as time passed by, and hurt her own children without a second thought. Things became worst as Papaw and Mamaw were granted custody and J.D. could visit his mother only when he chose to do so.

As if J.D.'s struggles were not enough, he was heartbroken when he found out that Lindsay – who he thought was the only "full sister" he had – was also a half-sister. Furthermore, his mother changed partners frequently after Bob – his legal father – divorced her, he slowly thought that they were never meant to stay. His mother had her own reasons for bringing all these men, but she also wanted someone to take care of and love her children as if his own. As a result of it all, Lindsay and Vance concluded the painful truth that they had no one to depend on.

Soon after Bev felt that Bob could no longer take the burden of an extra child, a man named Don Bowman – J.D.'s biological father – came back into their lives. After spending some time with his father, he realized that Don had changed for the better. He still argued with his wife, but it was nothing compared to the violence he witnessed before.

J.D. realized why his father had changed. Although his extended family thought Don was good for nothing, his religious views had guided him to lead a better life. As a result, J.D. evangelical theology became appealing to him but he also felt a growing mistrust against other segments of society.

In spite of his father's return, J.D. still held onto the bad memories since Don abandoned them. But upon realizing all the things his father had done to get his custody, the pain somehow subsided.

SEVEN

Losing the Anchor

Life continued the same for J.D. Just when he thought that the odds were finally on his side, a tragedy struck one day. When Mamaw called him to inquire about Papaw, he discerned that something was off. Papaw was a predictable man and his everyday routines were: woke up at the same time every morning, ate the same breakfast each day, stayed at Mamaw's place during the day, and greeted J.D. and Lindsay when they got home from school. However, this particular day, no one had seen or heard from Papaw, causing Mamaw to be hysterical.

When they reached Papaw's house, they found him slouched in his chair. The man who seemed to keep the whole family together, sane, and happy had already died.

Probably the most upsetting impact of losing Papaw was the fact that he was the only real father figure of J.D. Papaw was the one who taught him how to shoot properly, how to apologize through actions and not words, and how to protect and welcome the love from those their care about. He had been J.D.'s refuge when his mother was in a quarrel with her latest husband, that anchor was gone.

All the family members dealt differently with Papaw's death. Mamaw who put up bravery as a facade seemed lost. Lindsay spent most of her time with her friends to cope up with it. But the person who suffered the most was Bev. Her anger issues had worsened. She was quick to snap at others for their slightest mistakes, unleashing all her anger on anyone or anything. Moreover, she developed a serious drug addiction.

The children were left with no other choice than to stand on their own. Despite of the fact that Lindsay was only a high school graduate and J.D. was still in seventh grade, they managed to fend for themselves. Instead of being a burden to Mamaw, they relied on each other to solve their problems for Mamaw had spent most of her life dealing with one crisis or another. They even accompanied their mother in her rehab sessions to help her quit her addiction.

Eventually, she improved over time but she told her children that they should not judge her because according to her drug addiction was a disease. An uncontrollable disease just like cancer and any other illness, that she had no power over it. Of course, this logic did not appeal to them, but they knew that she was doing her best to put an end to her addiction, and together, they helped her overcome it.

EIGHT

No Fixed Abode

As the Vances moved on with their life, time healed all their wounds. J.D. was doing well in school; Mamaw had managed to take a vacation; Bev became sober; and ultimately, Lindsay got married to a wonderful man who treated her with so much respect she deserved. It was a breath of fresh air for the family, and J.D. could not have been more happy and content. In addition to this happy moment, Lindsay became pregnant within just one year of her marriage.

Just as J.D. thought that things were going to change for good, his mother announced that he had to move to Dayton to live with her and her newest boyfriend. He was furious about it, and as a result, his mother ordered him to see a therapist. His first session felt like an ambush because the therapist asked him about the outbursts he allegedly did when he was a child to which he could not remember. It was evident that the therapist based her impression of him from his mother's chronicles. Rather than working through his own problems, he lied to the therapist in order to protect his mother. He chose his words very carefully for he was afraid that any confession of his would send his mother straight to jail due to domestic violence.

Since J.D. did not want to stay with his mother, he decided to live with his father instead. But everyone was not happy with his decision. In some ways, he loved living with his father. Normal and perfect as his father's home to him – no adults fighting, slapping, and screaming –, its sense of uncertainty gave him an uneasy feeling. He also did not know his father quite enough to discuss anything with him, and so he went back home and lived with Mamaw.

Mamaw welcomed him with open arms and made him feel that he belonged there. But it was clear to him that she was too weak and exhausted to look after a teenager.

He had no choice but to return to his mother and Matt in Dayton. They were constantly fighting and finally, they ended their relationship. Then she met Ken, her boss in a local dialysis center, and their relationship was moving too fast. He asked her to dinner one night, and then she agreed to marry him a week later. Moreover, they moved into Ken's house shortly. It was his fourth home in just two years.

Ken was born in Korea who had three children. The eldest of them had a constant fight with J.D.'s mother and even called her a bitch one night. Upon hearing this, J.D. had beaten his new stepbrother badly in return. Therefore, the two stepbrothers needed to be separated and J.D. was once again back with Mamaw.

J.D.'s became miserable mainly because of the constant moving and fighting, and the seemingly endless carousel of new faces he had to meet and learn to love.

NINE

Moving Back to Mamaw

In addition to J.D.'s miseries, Bev struggled with addiction once more. He finally reached his breaking point when she ordered him to give her a jar of clean urine. She did it out of her desperation to pass a drug test and keep her nursing license. Even Mamaw asked him to do so in order to save her daughter from the law and convinced him that she would finally learn her lesson. Although against his will, he complied with his grandmother.

After that incident, Mamaw insisted that J.D. should stay with her permanently. As moving from one house to another was really tough for him, he agreed with her once more. Although he loved living with her, his new home tested his patience in many levels. They also had a set of house rules: get good grades, get a job, and "get off your ass and help me." No matter how hard she treated him, he enjoyed his time with her. She was constantly reminding him about the importance of education. But at some point, he was so close to dropping out of school and he did not have the guts to bring up the matter to her.

As tough as she was, Mamaw was very supportive especially to J.D.'s education. She even spent $180 for his graphing calculator despite of her financial situation. This had inspired J.D. to take schoolwork seriously. He spent three wonderful years with her and that was the turning point of his life. He got better grades, and he made some new friends. He also started working at a grocery store upon Mamaw's insistence.

While their lives were heading in the right direction, the immigrants in Ohio had the same problems – shouting matches, child abuse, shirking work due to laziness, and drug-related issues – they had suffered back in Kentucky. It was heartbreaking to see the people who tried to escape those things had followed them. J.D. pondered the question on why all these problems continued to exist in their community. In answer to his own question, he realized that while their elegy was a sociological one; the community, their faith, and the psychology played significant roles too.

TEN

Beating the Odds

After finishing high school and with his friends headed to college, he figured he would do the same. He scored well enough in SAT exams and made a decision to settle either Miami University or Ohio State. His excitement turned to apprehension for he was clueless about the whole process. He doubted his capabilities and could not shake the feeling that he had a long way to go. Everything about college responsibilities terrified him– from feeding himself to paying his own bills. But he wanted to excel in college, land a good job, and provide for his family. Life has so many amazing things to offer if he would just have the courage to face it. But he was not just ready to start his college journey.

During that time, his cousin Rachael – a Marine Corps veteran – suggested that he should enlist in the Marine Corps. They achieved great renown for shaping young boys into disciplined men. Four years in the Marines, he thought would mold him to the person he ought to be. Weeks later, he signed his name on a dotted line and left for camp. Mamaw was completely against his decision but she still supported him by sending letters of love and encouragement. Despite the severity of military life and training, he surprised himself by doing the things he thought was impossible. After he returned home, it was evident that everybody was treating him with reverence. Joining the Marine Corps gave him the perspective to see what he was capable of in life.

As Mamaw got older, her health began to deteriorate. She slipped into a coma and passed away. J.D. lost more than a mother as she raised him to become a better man amidst all odds. She was the only person who had believed that he could achieve anything he desired. That very belief and his training at Corps changed his perspective on life.

With a new sense of self-determination, a broader perspective of the larger world, and developed leadership skills, J.D. enrolled at Ohio State University. His military training made him an invincible man. He wanted to be a lawyer and he worked extra hard for it, hence he was working with two jobs. Despite his busy schedule, he still managed to maintain his social life. Finally after years of multitasking, studying and working, he graduated. While he had an incredible momentum, the working-class whites still had the same passive lifestyles.

He was very ecstatic when he received a call stating that his application to Yale was accepted. Yale was a student's wonderland. Professors encouraged their students to pursue their dreams and there was no pressure regarding their grades. Yale had a lot of great things to offer but J.D. felt as if he did not belong there. He could not fit into the "Yale elites." Although he felt his life story offered nothing exciting, his friends and professors found his roots incredibly fascinating.

Instead of a usual job interview, a dinner was hosted by Gibson Dunn and people networked over cocktails and dinner. The interviewers did not count credentials and résumés as advantages, but social standing had leverage. Successful people networked, emailed friends asking for favors, had their interviews set well in advance, and even listened to parents who instructed them about everything including the way they dressed, talked and carried themselves. But for a young man who had a poor background, J.D. had learned the hard way after messing up in an interview. Fortunately, his referrers had already put in a good word for him, and it saved him. Social capital was a paramount resource to be used, and if it weren't for Yale, he would not have been educated about so many things about which he was previously unaware.

Yale became more bearable when J.D. met Usha and fell head over heels for her. Everything seemed great for him, and with his beautiful girlfriend life started to become blissful. However, some of his Appalachian traits had not been eradicated. Whenever he disagreed with Usha, he thought of withdrawing from it or starting a shouting match. Unlike most hillbillies, he felt it was better to run away from it than to display his Appalachian outburst. He also realized that he was behaving just like her mother. He considered going to a psychologist but could not bring himself to talk about his personal issues with a stranger. Instead, he had read books which offered him a lot of insight, and he discovered that he was suffering from

ACEs – adverse childhood experiences. He conducted further research about ACEs, and he found out that children suffering from it not only had a higher risk of contracting cancer, but they were also more likely to become obese, and to underperform in any activities they took up. Along with this, however, came the realization that not everything was doomed. All he needed was someone to talk to – someone who understood him – and the more he thought about becoming like his mother, the more he tried to finally understand her.

After he graduated from Yale Law School, J.D and Usha got married and they bought a home in Cincinnati. He had a decent job, and ultimately he lived the American Dream. Some things remained the same such as his mother's addiction. It finally seemed like she had no hope for a better future but J.D. could not just walk away from his mother so he still did his best to help her.

The path to the American Dream was not an easy ride for J.D. His past experiences seemed like a recipe for disaster for his future self but his family knew better. He had the good fortune to have some people in his life that truly loved him and tried to help him. While immersed in a culture of poverty and drugs, he was able to find somewhat of a safe but poor haven. He sought out and took advice from several people whom he trusted who guided him at certain critical stages in his life. He was able to extricate himself from his hillbilly world and become a lawyer with a very positive personal life and career.

ELEVEN

Takeaways and Analysis

If there is one main key takeaway from reading this book, it should be empathy. It is likely that J.D.'s story represents both the low end of hillbilly culture with the drug addicted mother, revolving door father-figures, and unawareness of the outside world. At the same time, it also portrays an atypical result where someone was able to overcome the difficult start and had the talent to make it to and graduate from Yale's law school. However, the domestic abuse and social stigma he dealt with should work to kill some of the unforgiving dismissal of hicks, bumpkins, and swamp people that are common in suburban and urban culture.

Just as telling the chronicles of ethnic minorities suffering simply because of their ethnicity are part of the narrative of identity politics on the left, so might listening to stories of legitimate hardship among the many white, rural poor are a necessary part of understanding the perspective of a large swath of the nation.

At the same time, many more cosmopolitan Americans still fail to realize that being among the rural poor can be nearly as socially damning as being an ethnic minority, but without the protection of the media, the judicial system, and the cultural left. Hillbilly Elegy helps explain why some people don't believe in "White Privilege" and think that affirmative action is a form of vile racism. They feel like they are on the bottom of the social ladder and the zero-sum game policies of the political left keep them down. In some cases, that's likely the case. As J.D. explains, being white does not grant as much social capital as those who equate whiteness with established families and well-positioned social networks seem to believe. It is not that there is no benefit in some segments of society to being white, but that it is not quite the ticket to an easy life that some seem to describe.

Hillbilly Elegy does not answer every question about the white working class and its struggles. However, this memoir of a kid who endured a rough childhood but is doing pretty well so far helps to give a view into a world that many people never see from the interstates. It challenges racial narratives and, if read for empathy's sake, could break down some of the bubble many appear to live in.

Synopsis

J.D.'s unapologetic autobiography, "Hillbilly Elegy: A Memoir of a Family and Culture in Crisis," is a poem to the hills and hollers of his childhood where a blue-collar sentiment often blames government and big business for poverty, addiction, violence and families in disarray. The book echoes with an insider's righteousness of a boy — weaned on the cursing and strength of his Mamaw — who grows up to reject that defeatist mind-set by enlisting in the Marines and graduating from Yale Law School.

About the Author

J.D. Vance grew up in the Rust Belt city of Middletown, Ohio, and the Appalachian town of Jackson, Kentucky. He enlisted in the Marine Corps after high school and served in Iraq. A graduate of the Ohio State University and Yale Law School, he has contributed to the National Review and is a principal at a leading Silicon Valley investment firm. Vance lives in San Francisco with his wife and two dogs.

Made in the USA
Monee, IL
22 July 2024

62414390R00024